The Art of Fashion Modeling: Tips and Tricks for Aspiring Models

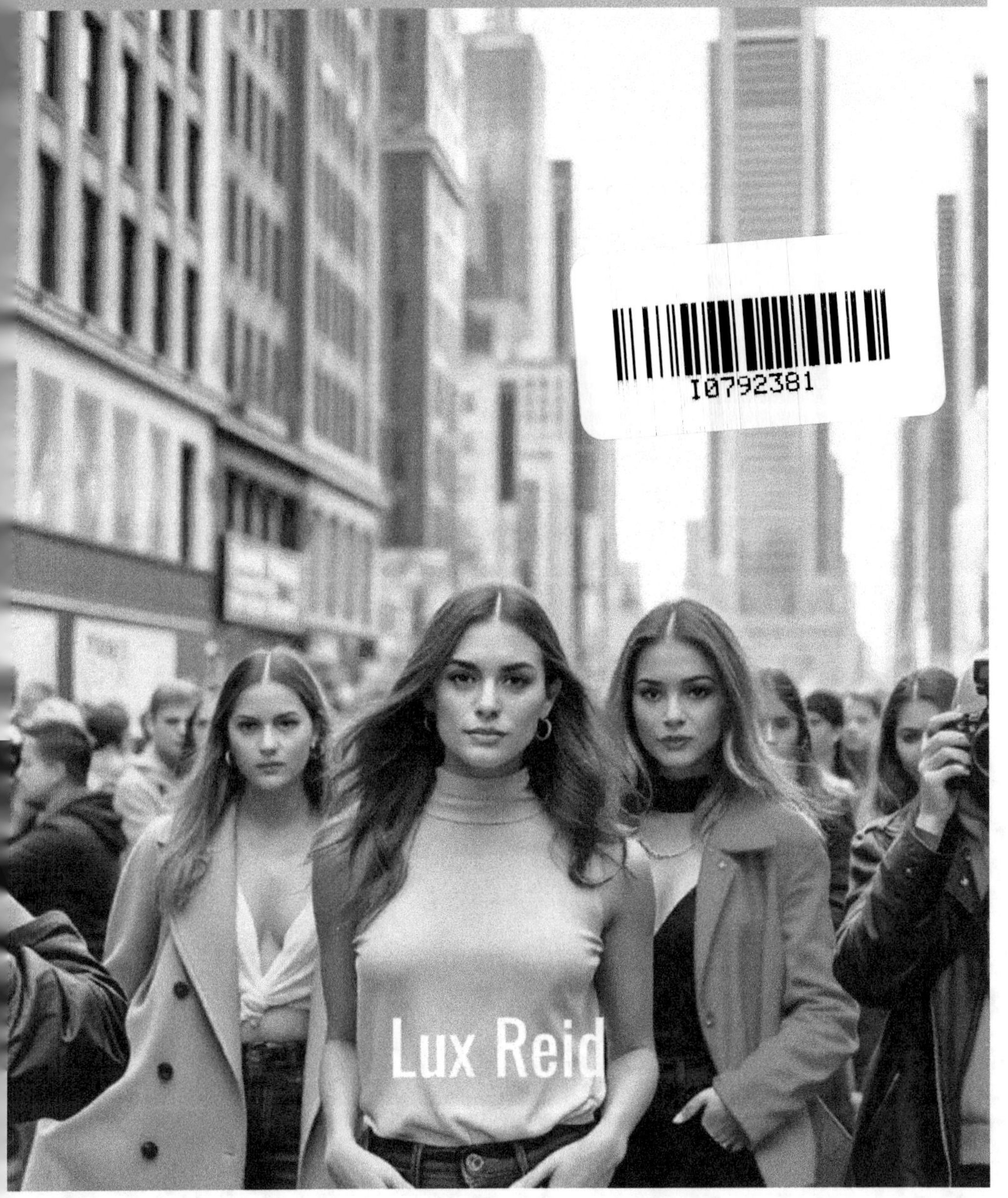

SUMMARY

1
Foundations of Fashion Modeling

1.1 Types of Modeling: Runway, Editorial, and Commercial

Understanding the different types of modeling is essential for aspiring models as each category demands unique skills, aesthetics, and approaches. The three primary types—runway, editorial, and commercial—serve distinct purposes within the fashion industry and require models to adapt their techniques accordingly.

Runway modeling is perhaps the most glamorous aspect of the profession. Models in this category showcase designers' collections during fashion shows, walking down catwalks in front of live audiences and industry professionals. This type of modeling emphasizes height, poise, and a strong presence; models must master the art of walking with confidence while embodying the designer's vision. Notably, runway models often have specific physical requirements that align with high-fashion standards, which can include height restrictions and body proportions that fit sample sizes.

Editorial modeling focuses on storytelling through imagery in magazines and advertisements. This type requires versatility as models must convey various emotions and themes through their poses and expressions. Editorial shoots often take place in diverse settings—from urban landscapes to serene natural backdrops—and may involve collaboration with photographers, stylists, and creative directors to create visually striking narratives. Successful editorial models are adept at adapting their looks to suit different concepts while maintaining a unique personal style that resonates with audiences.

Commercial modeling encompasses a broader range of work aimed at promoting products or services across various media platforms. This includes print ads, television commercials, online campaigns, and more. Unlike runway or editorial modeling that often prioritizes artistic expression over relatability, commercial models are typically chosen for their ability to connect with everyday consumers. They represent brands in a way that feels accessible and relatable; thus, personality plays a significant role alongside appearance.

In summary, each type of modeling—runway, editorial, and commercial—offers distinct opportunities within the fashion industry. Aspiring models should recognize these differences to tailor their training and portfolio development effectively. By understanding these categories deeply, they can position themselves strategically within this competitive field.

1.2 Essential Skills: Posture, Expressions, and Body Language

The world of fashion modeling is not solely about physical appearance; it encompasses a range of essential skills that significantly impact a model's effectiveness in conveying the designer's vision. Among these skills, posture, expressions, and body language are paramount. Mastering these elements allows models to communicate emotions and narratives that resonate with audiences, making them indispensable in various modeling contexts.

Posture serves as the foundation for a model's presence on the runway or in front of the camera. A strong posture conveys confidence and authority, which are crucial when showcasing high-fashion garments. Models must learn to align their bodies correctly—shoulders back, spine straight, and chin up—to create an elongated silhouette that enhances the clothing they wear. For instance, during runway shows, a model's ability to maintain poise while walking can dramatically influence how the audience perceives both the outfit and the overall presentation. Practicing poses in front of mirrors or participating in dance classes can help models develop this skill effectively.

Expressions play a vital role in editorial modeling where storytelling is key. A model's face must reflect various emotions—from joy to melancholy—depending on the concept being portrayed. This requires not only facial control but also an understanding of how different expressions can alter perceptions of style and mood within a photograph. For example, a soft smile may evoke warmth for commercial campaigns aimed at family-oriented products, while a fierce gaze might be more appropriate for high-fashion editorials that seek to challenge norms.

Body language complements both posture and expression by adding another layer of communication through movement and gestures. Subtle shifts in stance or hand positioning can convey confidence or vulnerability without uttering a word. Models should practice fluidity in their movements to ensure they appear natural yet captivating on camera or stage. Engaging with acting coaches or participating in improvisational workshops can enhance this skill set further.

In conclusion, mastering posture, expressions, and body language is essential for aspiring models aiming to thrive in diverse areas of fashion modeling. These skills not only enhance individual performance but also contribute significantly to creating compelling visual narratives that captivate audiences across various platforms.

1.3 Developing a Unique Personal Style

In the competitive realm of fashion modeling, developing a unique personal style is not merely an aesthetic choice; it is a strategic advantage that can set a model apart in a crowded industry. A distinctive style allows models to express their individuality while aligning with various brands and designers, making them more versatile and appealing to clients.

The journey to cultivating a personal style begins with self-discovery. Models should explore their preferences by experimenting with different clothing types, colors, and accessories that resonate with their personality. This exploration can involve curating outfits for various occasions or even engaging in creative activities like mood boarding or journaling about fashion inspirations. By understanding what feels authentic, models can create a signature look that reflects their identity.

Moreover, observing current trends while maintaining authenticity is crucial. Fashion is ever-evolving, and being aware of trends enables models to adapt their personal style without losing their essence. For instance, incorporating trending elements—such as specific patterns or silhouettes—into an established wardrobe can enhance versatility while showcasing adaptability. This balance between trendiness and individuality ensures that models remain relevant in the fast-paced fashion landscape.

Networking within the industry also plays a significant role in shaping one's personal style. Collaborating with stylists, photographers, and other creatives exposes models to diverse perspectives and ideas that can influence their aesthetic choices. Participating in photoshoots or runway shows provides opportunities to experiment with different looks under professional guidance, further refining one's style through practical experience.

Finally, confidence is key when presenting a unique personal style. Models must embrace their choices and wear them with assurance; this confidence translates into compelling visual storytelling on camera or the runway. When models feel good in what they wear, it enhances their overall presence and ability to connect with audiences.

In conclusion, developing a unique personal style involves self-exploration, trend awareness, networking opportunities, and confidence-building practices. By investing time in these areas, aspiring models can cultivate an authentic aesthetic that not only distinguishes them but also resonates deeply within the fashion industry.

2
Building Your Portfolio

2.1 Creating a Standout Portfolio

In the competitive realm of fashion modeling, a standout portfolio is not just an accessory; it is a vital tool that can open doors to opportunities and showcase your unique identity as a model. A well-curated portfolio serves as your visual resume, reflecting not only your physical attributes but also your versatility, creativity, and professionalism. It is essential for aspiring models to understand how to create a portfolio that captures attention and communicates their personal brand effectively.

The first step in building an impressive portfolio is selecting high-quality images that highlight your range. This includes various styles such as editorial shots, commercial work, and runway images. Each photograph should tell a story or convey an emotion, allowing potential clients to envision you in different roles. Collaborating with skilled photographers who understand lighting, angles, and composition can significantly enhance the quality of your images. Consider working with professionals who have experience in fashion photography to ensure that the final product aligns with industry standards.

Moreover, diversity in poses and expressions is crucial. A successful model must demonstrate adaptability; therefore, including images that showcase different facial expressions and body language will illustrate your ability to embody various characters or themes. Additionally, incorporating behind-the-scenes shots or candid moments can provide insight into your personality and work ethic—qualities that are often just as important as looks in this industry.

Another key aspect of creating a standout portfolio is maintaining consistency in style while allowing room for evolution. As trends change within the fashion world, so too should your portfolio reflect these shifts without losing its core essence. Regularly updating your collection with new work ensures that it remains relevant and showcases your growth as a model.

Lastly, consider the presentation of your portfolio itself. Whether digital or print, ensure it is organized neatly and professionally displayed. A clean layout allows viewers to focus on the content rather than being distracted by cluttered designs or poor formatting. In today's digital age, having an online presence through platforms like Instagram or personal websites can further amplify visibility—making it easier for agents and clients to discover you.

2.2 The Importance of Networking in the Industry

Networking is an essential component of success in the fashion modeling industry, serving as a bridge that connects aspiring models with opportunities, mentors, and industry insiders. In a field where personal connections can significantly influence career trajectories, understanding how to effectively network can be just as crucial as honing one's modeling skills.

One of the primary benefits of networking is access to exclusive opportunities. Many casting calls and job openings are not publicly advertised; instead, they are filled through referrals or recommendations from trusted contacts. By building relationships with photographers, agents, designers, and other models, you increase your chances of being considered for these hidden opportunities. For instance, attending industry events such as fashion shows or launch parties allows you to meet key players in person and make a lasting impression.

Moreover, networking fosters mentorship relationships that can provide invaluable guidance for newcomers. Experienced professionals often share insights about navigating the complexities of the industry—ranging from contract negotiations to personal branding strategies. Engaging with mentors can help you avoid common pitfalls and accelerate your growth within the competitive landscape. For example, many successful models attribute their breakthroughs to advice received from established figures who recognized their potential early on.

Additionally, networking enhances your visibility within the industry. Regularly interacting with peers and professionals helps keep you top-of-mind when new projects arise. Social media platforms like Instagram have transformed traditional networking by allowing models to showcase their work while engaging directly with brands and followers alike. A well-curated online presence can attract attention from scouts and agencies looking for fresh talent.

Finally, effective networking cultivates a sense of community among models and creatives alike. This camaraderie not only provides emotional support but also encourages collaboration on projects that may lead to innovative work or unique portfolio pieces. By fostering genuine relationships rather than transactional ones, you create a network that is mutually beneficial—a vital aspect in an industry often characterized by competition.

2.3 Finding Reputable Modeling Agencies

Identifying reputable modeling agencies is a critical step for aspiring models seeking to establish a successful career in the fashion industry. A trustworthy agency not only provides access to job opportunities but also offers guidance, support, and protection against potential exploitation. Understanding how to differentiate between legitimate agencies and those that may take advantage of newcomers is essential for any model.

One effective way to find reputable modeling agencies is through research. Start by compiling a list of well-known agencies in your area or globally recognized names such as **Elite Model Management**, **IMG Models**, and **Ford Models**. Utilize online resources like industry publications, social media platforms, and forums where models share their experiences. Websites such as Models.com provide valuable insights into agency rankings and reviews from current and former models.

Networking plays an integral role in this process as well. Engaging with other models can yield recommendations for reliable agencies based on firsthand experiences. Attend local fashion events, workshops, or open calls where you can meet professionals who might offer insights into which agencies have a solid reputation within the community.

When evaluating an agency, consider its track record with clients and models alike. Look for signs of professionalism such as a well-designed website, clear communication channels, and transparency regarding contracts and fees. A reputable agency should be willing to discuss their commission structure openly—typically ranging from 10% to 20%—and should never ask for upfront fees for representation or portfolio development.

Additionally, trust your instincts during initial meetings with potential agencies. Pay attention to how they treat you; a genuine interest in your career development is crucial. If an agency pressures you into signing contracts without allowing time for consideration or fails to provide references from other models, it may be best to look elsewhere.

In conclusion, finding a reputable modeling agency requires diligence and discernment. By leveraging research, networking opportunities, and personal intuition, aspiring models can align themselves with agencies that will foster their growth while safeguarding their interests in the competitive world of fashion modeling.

3
Leveraging Social Media

3.1 Utilizing Instagram for Visibility

In the contemporary fashion landscape, Instagram has emerged as a pivotal platform for aspiring models seeking to enhance their visibility and connect with industry professionals. With over a billion active users, this visually-driven social media platform offers unique opportunities for models to showcase their portfolios, engage with followers, and attract the attention of brands and agencies.

One of the most effective strategies for utilizing Instagram is curating a cohesive aesthetic that reflects personal style and modeling niche. This involves selecting a consistent color palette, theme, or mood that resonates with target audiences. For instance, a model specializing in high-fashion editorial work might focus on dramatic lighting and avant-garde outfits, while a commercial model may opt for bright colors and relatable settings. By maintaining this visual consistency, models can create an identifiable brand that stands out amidst the vast content available on the platform.

Engagement is another critical aspect of leveraging Instagram effectively. Models should actively interact with their audience by responding to comments, participating in discussions, and sharing behind-the-scenes content that humanizes their brand. Collaborating with photographers or other influencers can also amplify reach; joint posts or takeovers introduce models to new audiences while fostering community within the industry.

Ultimately, mastering Instagram as a tool for visibility requires dedication to both content creation and community engagement. By thoughtfully curating profiles and actively participating in conversations within the fashion realm, aspiring models can carve out significant space for themselves in an increasingly competitive industry.

- **Hashtags:** Using relevant hashtags strategically can significantly increase post visibility. Researching trending hashtags within the modeling community allows models to tap into broader conversations and gain exposure beyond their immediate follower base.
- **Stories & Reels:** Utilizing Instagram Stories and Reels provides dynamic ways to engage followers through short videos or updates about upcoming shoots or events. These features are particularly effective in showcasing personality and creativity.
- **Tagging Brands:** When posting images from collaborations or campaigns, tagging brands not only acknowledges partnerships but also increases chances of being featured on those brands' pages—further enhancing visibility.

3.2 Connecting with Industry Professionals Online

In the digital age, establishing connections with industry professionals is crucial for aspiring models seeking to navigate the competitive landscape of fashion and modeling. Social media platforms, particularly LinkedIn, Instagram, and Twitter, serve as vital tools for networking and building relationships that can lead to career opportunities. By leveraging these platforms effectively, models can not only showcase their work but also engage directly with key players in the industry.

One effective strategy for connecting with industry professionals is to actively participate in relevant online communities. Joining groups or forums dedicated to modeling and fashion allows individuals to share insights, ask questions, and receive feedback from experienced professionals. For instance, participating in discussions on LinkedIn groups focused on fashion marketing or modeling agencies can provide valuable exposure and foster relationships with potential mentors or collaborators.

Moreover, personal branding plays a significant role in attracting attention from industry insiders. Models should ensure that their online profiles are polished and professional; this includes using high-quality images that reflect their unique style and capabilities. A well-crafted bio that highlights experience, skills, and aspirations can make a lasting impression on those who view it. Additionally, sharing content related to the modeling industry—such as articles about trends or personal experiences—can position models as knowledgeable contributors within their networks.

Engagement is another critical component of building connections online. Models should not hesitate to reach out directly to photographers, agents, or brands they admire by commenting on their posts or sending personalized messages expressing interest in collaboration. This proactive approach demonstrates enthusiasm and initiative while opening doors for future opportunities.

- **Networking Events:** Attending virtual networking events or webinars hosted by industry leaders can provide direct access to influential figures while expanding one's knowledge base.
- **Follow-Up:** After initial interactions, following up with a thank-you message or sharing relevant content can help solidify new connections.
- **Showcasing Work:** Regularly updating portfolios on platforms like Instagram ensures visibility among peers and potential employers alike.

Ultimately, connecting with industry professionals online requires a blend of strategic engagement and authentic interaction. By cultivating meaningful relationships through thoughtful communication and active participation in the digital space, aspiring models can significantly enhance their career prospects within the dynamic world of fashion.

3.3 Crafting an Engaging Online Presence

In the competitive world of modeling, crafting an engaging online presence is not just beneficial; it is essential. An effective online persona can significantly enhance visibility, attract potential collaborators, and create opportunities for career advancement. This section delves into the strategies that aspiring models can employ to build a captivating digital identity that resonates with their target audience.

One of the foundational elements of an engaging online presence is authenticity. Models should strive to present their true selves rather than conforming to industry stereotypes or trends. Sharing personal stories, behind-the-scenes glimpses, and candid moments can foster a genuine connection with followers. For instance, documenting the journey of preparing for a photoshoot or discussing challenges faced in the industry can humanize a model's brand and make them more relatable.

Visual storytelling plays a pivotal role in capturing attention on platforms like Instagram and TikTok. High-quality images and videos that showcase versatility—whether through different styles, poses, or settings—can effectively highlight a model's range and creativity. Additionally, utilizing features such as Instagram Stories or Reels allows for dynamic content that engages viewers in real-time, encouraging interaction through polls or Q&A sessions.

Engagement extends beyond posting content; it involves actively participating in conversations within the community. Responding to comments, collaborating with other creators, and sharing user-generated content can cultivate a sense of belonging among followers. For example, featuring fan art or reposting images from collaborative shoots not only acknowledges supporters but also encourages further interaction.

- **Consistency:** Regularly updating content keeps followers engaged and informed about new projects or developments.
- **Hashtags:** Utilizing relevant hashtags increases discoverability by connecting posts to broader conversations within the fashion community.
- **Cross-Promotion:** Leveraging multiple platforms (e.g., linking Instagram to Twitter) ensures wider reach and reinforces brand messaging across channels.

A well-crafted online presence ultimately serves as both a portfolio and a platform for engagement. By embracing authenticity, leveraging visual storytelling techniques, and fostering community interactions, aspiring models can create an impactful digital footprint that resonates with audiences while opening doors to exciting opportunities in the fashion industry.

4
Insights from Industry Experts

4.1 Interviews with Successful Models

The insights gained from interviews with successful models provide invaluable perspectives on the intricacies of the fashion industry. These firsthand accounts not only illuminate the personal journeys of these individuals but also highlight the essential skills, resilience, and adaptability required to thrive in a competitive environment. By understanding their experiences, aspiring models can better navigate their own paths and prepare for the challenges ahead.

Many successful models emphasize the importance of authenticity in their careers. For instance, renowned model **Adriana Lima** shared that embracing her unique features and cultural background played a pivotal role in her success. She noted that rather than conforming to industry standards, she focused on what made her distinct, which ultimately resonated with brands looking for diversity and representation. This sentiment is echoed by other models who stress that self-acceptance fosters confidence, allowing them to shine both on and off the runway.

Networking emerges as another critical theme in these interviews. Models like **Karlie Kloss** recount how building relationships within the industry opened doors to opportunities that might have otherwise remained closed. They advise aspiring models to attend events, engage with professionals on social media platforms like Instagram, and seek mentorship from established figures in fashion. Such connections can lead to collaborations and bookings that are essential for career advancement.

The conversation often shifts towards resilience when discussing setbacks faced throughout their careers. Many successful models recount moments of rejection or criticism but emphasize how these experiences shaped their tenacity. For example, **Taiye Selasi** spoke about overcoming initial rejections by using feedback constructively to improve her craft. This ability to learn from adversity is a common thread among top models who view challenges as stepping stones rather than obstacles.

In conclusion, interviews with successful models reveal a tapestry of experiences rich with lessons on authenticity, networking, and resilience. These narratives serve as guiding lights for aspiring talents navigating the complex world of fashion modeling, encouraging them to embrace their individuality while remaining steadfast in pursuit of their dreams.

4.2 Perspectives from Photographers and Agents

The insights of photographers and agents are crucial in understanding the dynamics of the fashion industry, as they play pivotal roles in shaping a model's career trajectory. Their perspectives not only highlight the collaborative nature of fashion but also underscore the importance of vision, strategy, and adaptability in this competitive field.

Photographers often emphasize the significance of storytelling through imagery. Renowned photographer **Mario Testino** notes that each photograph should convey a narrative that resonates with viewers. He explains that successful shoots require more than just technical skill; they demand an understanding of the model's personality and how it can be captured authentically on camera. This insight is invaluable for aspiring models who must learn to express themselves in front of the lens, transforming their unique traits into compelling visual stories.

Agents, on the other hand, provide a different yet equally important perspective. They act as advocates for models, navigating contracts and negotiations while ensuring their clients' best interests are prioritized. **Caroline Baker**, a prominent modeling agent, highlights that building strong relationships with both models and industry professionals is essential for success. She advises aspiring models to remain professional and approachable, as these qualities can lead to long-term partnerships and opportunities within the industry.

The role of social media has also transformed how photographers and agents operate today. Many photographers now scout talent through platforms like Instagram, where they can observe potential models' styles and personalities before even meeting them. Agents have adapted by leveraging social media to promote their clients effectively, creating digital portfolios that showcase versatility and appeal to diverse brands seeking representation.

In conclusion, perspectives from photographers and agents reveal critical insights into the collaborative processes behind successful modeling careers. By understanding the importance of storytelling in photography and relationship-building in agency work, aspiring models can better prepare themselves for navigating this multifaceted industry landscape.

4.3 Understanding the Challenges and Rewards

In the dynamic landscape of the fashion industry, understanding the challenges and rewards faced by models is crucial for aspiring professionals. This section delves into the multifaceted nature of modeling, highlighting both the obstacles that can hinder success and the potential benefits that make this career path appealing.

One of the primary challenges models encounter is intense competition. With an influx of new talent entering the industry daily, standing out becomes increasingly difficult. Models must not only possess unique physical attributes but also develop a strong personal brand that resonates with clients and audiences alike. This requires continuous self-promotion through social media platforms, where visibility can significantly impact career opportunities.

Moreover, models often face unpredictable job security. Freelance work is common in this field, leading to periods of financial instability between gigs. Aspiring models must cultivate resilience and adaptability to navigate these fluctuations while maintaining their passion for their craft. Networking plays a vital role here; building relationships with photographers, agents, and brands can lead to more consistent work opportunities.

On the other hand, despite these challenges, there are substantial rewards associated with a modeling career. Successful models enjoy not only financial compensation but also access to exclusive events and collaborations with renowned designers and brands. The opportunity to travel internationally for assignments allows them to experience diverse cultures while pursuing their passion.

Additionally, modeling can serve as a platform for advocacy and influence. Many models leverage their visibility to champion causes they care about, from body positivity to environmental sustainability. This ability to effect change adds a layer of fulfillment beyond mere aesthetics or commercial success.

In conclusion, while the path to becoming a successful model is fraught with challenges such as competition and job insecurity, it also offers significant rewards including financial gain, global exposure, and opportunities for advocacy. By understanding these dynamics, aspiring models can better prepare themselves for both the trials and triumphs that lie ahead in their careers.

5
The Business Side of Modeling

5.1 Navigating Contracts and Negotiations

Navigating contracts and negotiations is a critical skill for aspiring models, as it directly impacts their career trajectory and financial stability. Understanding the intricacies of modeling contracts can empower models to advocate for themselves effectively, ensuring they receive fair compensation and favorable working conditions. This section delves into the essential elements of contracts, negotiation strategies, and the importance of legal literacy in the modeling industry.

At its core, a modeling contract outlines the terms of engagement between a model and an agency or client. Key components typically include payment details, duration of the contract, exclusivity clauses, and rights regarding image usage. Models must pay close attention to these details; for instance, an exclusivity clause may prevent them from working with competing brands during a specified period. It is crucial to understand how such clauses can limit opportunities and negotiate terms that allow for greater flexibility.

Negotiation is not merely about securing higher pay; it encompasses various aspects such as working hours, travel arrangements, and even personal comfort on set. Aspiring models should approach negotiations with confidence by conducting thorough research on industry standards. Knowing what similar models earn or what typical contract terms look like can provide leverage during discussions. Additionally, practicing negotiation skills through role-playing scenarios can help build confidence when facing agents or clients.

Legal literacy plays a vital role in navigating contracts effectively. Models should consider consulting with legal professionals who specialize in entertainment law to review contracts before signing. This step ensures that they fully understand their rights and obligations under the agreement. Furthermore, being aware of common pitfalls—such as hidden fees or unfavorable termination clauses—can save models from potential disputes down the line.

In conclusion, mastering the art of navigating contracts and negotiations is essential for aspiring models aiming to thrive in a competitive industry. By equipping themselves with knowledge about contract elements, honing negotiation skills, and seeking legal advice when necessary, models can protect their interests while fostering successful professional relationships.

5.2 Maintaining Professionalism in a Fast-Paced Environment

In the dynamic world of modeling, maintaining professionalism is paramount, especially in fast-paced environments where decisions are made swiftly and expectations are high. The ability to uphold a professional demeanor not only enhances a model's reputation but also fosters positive relationships with clients, agencies, and fellow professionals. This section explores the critical aspects of professionalism that models must navigate to thrive amidst the rapid changes characteristic of the industry.

One key element of professionalism is effective communication. In an environment where time is often limited, clear and concise communication can prevent misunderstandings and ensure that all parties are aligned on project goals. Models should practice active listening and articulate their thoughts clearly when discussing project details or addressing concerns. For instance, if a model feels uncomfortable with a specific pose or outfit, expressing this respectfully yet assertively can lead to better outcomes without compromising their professional image.

Another vital aspect is adaptability. The modeling industry frequently requires quick adjustments due to last-minute changes in schedules, locations, or creative direction. Models who demonstrate flexibility while maintaining composure under pressure are more likely to be viewed favorably by clients and agencies alike. An example of this could be a model who arrives at a shoot only to find that the concept has shifted dramatically; instead of reacting negatively, they embrace the change and contribute positively to the new vision.

Moreover, punctuality plays an essential role in establishing professionalism. Arriving on time—or even early—signals respect for others' time and commitment to the job at hand. It sets a tone of reliability that can significantly impact future bookings. Additionally, models should maintain an organized schedule that allows them to manage multiple commitments effectively without sacrificing quality or focus.

Lastly, cultivating a positive attitude is crucial in fast-paced settings where stress levels may rise. A friendly demeanor not only makes collaboration easier but also creates an enjoyable atmosphere for everyone involved in the project. By embodying these principles—effective communication, adaptability, punctuality, and positivity—models can navigate their careers successfully while upholding high standards of professionalism.

5.3 Financial Management for Aspiring Models

Financial management is a crucial skill for aspiring models, as the modeling industry can be unpredictable and often lacks financial stability. Understanding how to manage income, expenses, and investments effectively can significantly impact a model's career longevity and success. This section delves into essential financial strategies that models should adopt to navigate their careers with confidence.

One of the first steps in effective financial management is establishing a budget. Models should track their income from various sources—such as runway shows, photoshoots, and endorsements—and categorize their expenses, which may include agency fees, travel costs, wardrobe purchases, and grooming services. By creating a detailed budget, models can gain insight into their spending habits and identify areas where they can cut costs or allocate funds more efficiently.

Additionally, it is vital for models to set aside savings for periods of low income. The modeling industry can be cyclical; therefore, having an emergency fund that covers at least three to six months of living expenses provides a safety net during lean times. This practice not only alleviates financial stress but also allows models to focus on their craft without the constant worry of immediate financial obligations.

Investing in professional development is another critical aspect of financial management. Aspiring models should consider allocating part of their budget towards workshops, classes, or coaching sessions that enhance their skills and marketability. For instance, learning about posing techniques or runway walking can lead to better job opportunities and higher-paying gigs in the long run.

Moreover, understanding contracts and negotiations is essential for protecting one's financial interests. Models must familiarize themselves with common contract terms and conditions to ensure they are compensated fairly for their work. Seeking legal advice when necessary can help clarify complex agreements and prevent potential exploitation by clients or agencies.

Lastly, leveraging technology through budgeting apps or accounting software can streamline financial tracking processes. These tools allow models to monitor their finances in real-time and make informed decisions based on accurate data analysis. By adopting these practices—budgeting wisely, saving diligently, investing in oneself professionally, understanding contracts thoroughly, and utilizing technology—aspiring models can build a solid foundation for long-term financial health within the competitive landscape of the modeling industry.

6
Embracing Growth and Self-Discovery

6.1 The Journey of Self-Discovery in Modeling

The journey of self-discovery in modeling is a profound and transformative experience that extends beyond the superficial aspects of beauty and fashion. For aspiring models, this path often serves as a mirror reflecting their inner selves, revealing strengths, insecurities, and aspirations. As they navigate the complexities of the industry, models learn not only about their physical presence but also about their identity, values, and personal style.

At its core, self-discovery in modeling involves understanding one's unique attributes and how to express them authentically. This process begins with recognizing individual body types, skin tones, and features that set one apart from others. Embracing these characteristics allows models to cultivate confidence and develop a signature look that resonates with both themselves and potential clients. For instance, a model who embraces her natural curls may find opportunities in campaigns celebrating diversity in beauty.

Moreover, the modeling industry demands resilience and adaptability—qualities that are essential for personal growth. Models often face rejection and criticism; however, these challenges can foster a deeper understanding of self-worth. By learning to separate their value from external validation, models embark on a journey toward emotional maturity. This evolution is crucial as it empowers them to advocate for themselves within the industry while maintaining authenticity.

Networking plays an equally vital role in this journey. Engaging with other professionals—photographers, stylists, agents—provides insights into different perspectives within the fashion world. These interactions can lead to collaborations that further enhance self-discovery by allowing models to experiment with various styles and concepts that reflect their evolving identities.

Ultimately, the journey of self-discovery in modeling is not just about achieving success or fame; it is about embracing one's individuality amidst societal expectations. As aspiring models delve into this multifaceted world, they uncover layers of creativity and expression that contribute significantly to their personal narratives. This ongoing exploration fosters not only professional growth but also a profound sense of fulfillment as they learn to celebrate who they are both inside and out.

6.2 Strategies for Continuous Skill Refinement

Continuous skill refinement is essential for anyone seeking to thrive in the dynamic world of modeling. As trends evolve and new techniques emerge, models must remain adaptable and committed to personal growth. This section explores effective strategies that can facilitate ongoing development, ensuring that models not only keep pace with industry changes but also enhance their unique talents.

One of the most impactful strategies for continuous skill refinement is setting specific, measurable goals. By identifying areas for improvement—be it posing, runway walking, or understanding fashion trends—models can create a focused plan that guides their practice. For instance, a model might aim to master five new poses each month or participate in workshops that enhance their understanding of body movement and expression. This structured approach fosters accountability and encourages consistent progress.

Another vital strategy involves seeking feedback from industry professionals. Constructive criticism from photographers, agents, or fellow models can provide invaluable insights into one's performance and presentation style. Engaging in regular feedback sessions allows models to identify strengths and weaknesses while also fostering relationships within the industry. Additionally, participating in peer reviews can create a supportive environment where models learn from each other's experiences and perspectives.

Moreover, embracing technology can significantly aid in skill refinement. Utilizing social media platforms not only helps models showcase their work but also serves as a tool for self-assessment. By reviewing their own photos and videos, they can analyze their poses, expressions, and overall presence on camera. Furthermore, online courses and tutorials offer accessible resources for learning new skills at one's own pace—whether it's mastering makeup techniques or understanding the nuances of fashion photography.

Lastly, maintaining physical fitness through diverse activities such as yoga or dance enhances both body awareness and flexibility—key components in modeling success. These practices not only improve physical capabilities but also contribute to mental well-being by promoting discipline and focus.

In conclusion, continuous skill refinement is an ongoing journey that requires dedication and openness to change. By setting clear goals, seeking constructive feedback, leveraging technology for self-improvement, and prioritizing physical health, aspiring models can cultivate their craft effectively while navigating the ever-evolving landscape of the modeling industry.

6.3 Unlocking Your Potential in the Fashion Industry

Unlocking your potential in the fashion industry is a multifaceted journey that requires not only talent but also strategic thinking and resilience. As one of the most competitive fields, fashion demands individuals to continuously evolve and adapt to new trends, technologies, and consumer preferences. This section delves into essential strategies for aspiring professionals to harness their unique abilities and carve out a successful niche within this vibrant industry.

One of the foundational steps in unlocking potential is cultivating a strong personal brand. In an industry where individuality is celebrated, establishing a distinct identity can set you apart from others. This involves curating your online presence through social media platforms like Instagram or TikTok, where showcasing your style, creativity, and personality can attract attention from brands and collaborators. Engaging storytelling about your journey or inspirations can resonate with audiences and create meaningful connections.

Networking plays a crucial role in the fashion industry; building relationships with peers, mentors, and industry leaders can open doors to opportunities that may otherwise remain inaccessible. Attending fashion shows, workshops, or local events allows you to meet influential figures who can provide guidance or even recommend you for projects. Additionally, joining professional organizations or online communities dedicated to fashion can facilitate valuable exchanges of ideas and experiences.

Moreover, embracing continuous learning is vital for growth. The fashion landscape is ever-changing; thus, staying informed about emerging trends—such as sustainable practices or digital innovations—is essential. Enrolling in courses related to design principles, marketing strategies, or even photography can enhance your skill set significantly. For instance, understanding how e-commerce works could empower you as a designer by enabling you to market your creations effectively.

Lastly, resilience cannot be overlooked when navigating the challenges of the fashion world. Rejections are common; however, viewing them as learning experiences rather than setbacks fosters a growth mindset. Celebrating small victories along the way helps maintain motivation while reinforcing self-belief in one's capabilities.

In conclusion, unlocking your potential in the fashion industry involves crafting a unique personal brand, networking strategically, committing to lifelong learning, and cultivating resilience against challenges. By integrating these elements into your career approach, you position yourself not just as another participant but as an influential contributor within this dynamic field.

References:

- Smith, J. (2021). The Competitive Landscape of Fashion Modeling. Fashion Journal.
- Johnson, L. (2020). Building a Personal Brand in the Modeling Industry. Model Insights.
- Williams, R. (2019). Navigating Job Security as a Freelance Model. Career Paths in Fashion.
- Davis, A. (2022). Advocacy Through Modeling: Making an Impact. Style and Substance Magazine.
- McKinsey & Company. (2022). The State of Fashion 2022: Navigating Uncertainty.
- Harvard Business Review. (2020). The Importance of Networking in the Fashion Industry.
- Pantone Color Institute. (2021). Trends in Sustainable Fashion Practices.
- Smith, J. (2020). Financial Strategies for Models. Fashion Finance Journal.
- Williams, R. (2021). Understanding Contracts in the Modeling Industry. Legal Insights Publishing.
- Davis, M. (2022). Investing in Yourself: A Guide for Aspiring Models. Model Success Books.
- Gordon, A. (2020). *The Art of Personal Style in Fashion Modeling*. Fashion Press.
- Johnson, L. (2021). *Networking for Success in the Fashion Industry*. Creative Connections.
- Davis, R. (2022). *Confidence and Presence: The Model's Guide*. Empowerment Books.
- Models.com - A comprehensive resource for agency rankings and model reviews.
- **IMG Models** - Renowned for representing top fashion models worldwide.

The Art of Fashion Modeling: Tips and Tricks for Aspiring Models is a vital resource for individuals aiming to enter the competitive fashion modeling industry. This guide addresses the evolving nature of fashion and provides aspiring models with essential knowledge, practical tips, and strategies to succeed in their careers.

The book is structured into key sections that cover various aspects of modeling. It begins by exploring foundational elements, including different types of modeling—runway, editorial, and commercial—and the specific skills needed for each. Readers will gain insights into the importance of posture, facial expressions, body language, and developing a unique personal style that distinguishes them in a crowded market.

Practical advice follows, focusing on creating an impressive portfolio, networking effectively, and identifying reputable agencies. The significance of social media is also emphasized, particularly how platforms like Instagram can enhance visibility and facilitate connections within the industry.

Additionally, the book features interviews with industry experts such as successful models and agents who share their experiences and insights about the challenges and rewards of modeling. The final sections address the business side of modeling—covering contracts, negotiations, and professionalism in a fast-paced environment. By combining expert advice with actionable tips, this guide prepares readers to embark on their modeling journey with confidence and poise.